RAIL 11 PORTFOLIOS

The 56s and 58s

Paul Shannon

First published 1989

ISBN 0 7110 1853 7

© Ian Allan Ltd 1989

Published by

IAN ALLAN LTD

Terminal House Shepperton TW17 8AS
Telephone: Walton-on-Thames (0932) 228950
Fax: 0932 232366   Telex: 929806 IALLAN G
Registered Office: Terminal House Shepperton TW17 8AS
Printed by Butler & Tanner Ltd, Frome and London

Front cover: In grimy, workstained 'large logo' blue livery Class 56 No 56119 is seen at Butterwell Coal Loading Site with an MGR coal working to Blyth power station on 30 April 1987.   *Peter J. Robinson Pentax 6×7 105mm Takumar Ektachrome 200 1/125 f8-11*

Rear cover: Class 58 No 58041 takes the dive-under line at Retford with a loaded MGR train for West Burton power station on 17 August 1988.   *David Moulden Nikkormat FTN 50mm Nikkor Kodachrome 25 1/500 f2.8*

Right: Class 58 meets Class 56 near Castle Gresley, on the Coalville line, on 6 August 1987. The locomotives are No 58030 and No 56081, hauling a westbound loaded MGR and eastbound empties respectively. The cooling towers visible on the horizon belong to the huge Drakelow CEGB complex, which receives about three million tonnes of railborne coal per annum.
*Andrew Fell
Mamiya M645J 80mm Sekor C Ektachrome 64 1/500 f4*

Introduction

On 4 August 1976 British Rail took delivery of its first new diesel locomotive for nearly a decade. Although outwardly similar to the successful Brush Type 4 (later Class 47) of the 1960s, the Class 56 was conceived from the outset as a specialist freight locomotive, with the emphasis on traction capability rather than the attainment of high speeds. The impetus for the Class 56 building programme came from an anticipated upsurge in coal traffic following the rapidly rising oil prices of the mid-1970s. So urgent was BR's need that the first 30 locomotives were constructed by Electroputere in Romania, the only firm that could deliver the product within the required time. In the event the increased coal traffic was slow to materialise, which was perhaps just as well since the early '56s' were beset with faults and their entry into revenue-earning service was much delayed.

Construction of the remaining 105 locomotives in the fleet was shared between BREL's works at Doncaster and Crewe, with the former location attracting the lion's share of the work. Originally there was to have been a total of 170 Class 56s, but the final batch was curtailed by 35 in early 1982 in favour of an entirely new design — enter the Class 58! This design incorporated many new features and, most important of all, each locomotive turned out to be 15% cheaper to build than the equivalent Class 56. The fleet of Class 58s comprises the 35 'diverted' from the Class 56 order, plus a further 15, all constructed by BREL at Doncaster Works.

In this volume we depict Classes 56 and 58 in a variety of colour schemes and in a variety of settings. In barely more than a decade Class 56 locomotives have carried standard blue, revised blue (often referred to as 'large logo'), early Railfreight (mid grey) and new Railfreight (two-tone grey) liveries, and even within these categories detail variations have occurred. A far cry from the uniformity of the 1970s! The Class 58 fleet is visually more uniform, since these locomotives never carried blue but were outshopped right from the start in Railfreight grey. The sphere of operations of Class 56, too, has been more varied than that of Class 58. In addition to the merry-go-round (MGR) coal duties for which both classes were primarily intended, Class 56 traction is predominant on aggregates flows from the Midlands and the Mendip Hills, and has appeared regularly over the years on bulk steel, iron ore, oil, cement and Freightliner services. Class 58 diagrams, on the other hand, have rarely strayed beyond the confines of the MGR operation. Now that BR is firmly committed to dedicated locomotive fleets for specific commodities and services, Classes 56 and 58 are expected to specialise increasingly in the movement of coal and aggregates, although there will always be occasions when their use elsewhere is required.

The compiler and Publisher wish to thank the many photographers who contributed to this volume, helping to provide a many-sided view of BR's two newest and most powerful diesel locomotive classes. Until the Class 60, that is . . .

Paul Shannon
St Albans
October 1988

Below: After a freak snowfall in the picturesque Wylye Valley, Class 56 No 56041 heads the daily Ardingly-Whatley stone empties near Great Wishford on 20 March 1987. *Brian Denton*
Nikon FM   50mm   Kodachrome 64   1/500 f5.6

Left: In the heart of the Yorkshire coalfield, two-tone liveried Class 56 No 56015 passes Skellow Junction with an eastbound MGR train on 2 March 1988. Taking the curve to Carcroft Junction is a train of empties, headed by sister locomotive No 56097. The stretch of line between Skellow and Stainforth sees no passenger service but is kept busy with MGR workings to Thorpe Marsh power station and miscellaneous through freight services. *Hugh Ballantyne Leica M4-2 90mm Summicron Kodachrome 25 1/500 f2-2.8*

Right: The sidings on the north side of the Healey Mills yard complex are used for stabling MGR and other freight services waiting for a change of locomotive or crew. On 18 September 1984, Nos 56103 and 56099 each stand at the head of a rake of empty HAAs, whilst the left-hand siding houses a row of Class 40s, 37s and 31s. *John S. Whiteley Pentax SP1000 135mm Takumar Kodachrome 64 1/250 f4.5*

Left: Class 56 No 56003 passes Bedlington, in the depths of the Blyth and Tyne network, with the 6B15 MGR train from Swalwell to Blyth on the evening of 21 August 1987. At the time of writing there are seven Class 56 diagrams based on Blyth, all dedicated to Coal sub-Sector work.
Michael Rhodes
Canon AE-1 100mm Canon Kodachrome 64
1/250 f4-5.6

Above: Painted in 'red stripe' Railfreight livery, Class 56 No 56011 passes Clay Cross on the up goods line with loaded HAAs on 22 August 1988. The train is 7O34, the 17.04 Oxcroft-Ridham Dock, conveying fuel for the Bowaters paper factory at Sittingbourne. *Paul Shannon*
Olympus OM1 50mm Zuiko Kodachrome 64
1/250 f4-5.6

Left: Although now without its own allocation of locomotives, Knottingley depot remains active as a day-to-day base for Coal sub-Sector traction in the Aire Valley district. Standing outside the depot on 25 September 1986 are Class 56s Nos 56075 *West Yorkshire Enterprise* and 56095, painted in 'old' Railfreight grey and 'large logo' livery respectively. Appropriately enough, the skyline is dominated by the massive cooling towers of Ferrybridge power station. *Gavin Morrison*
Minolta 7000 Fujichrome 100 1/250 f8

Right: On the day of its naming, 9 July 1985, No 56075 *West Yorkshire Enterprise* poses for the photographer in the yard at Healey Mills. This locomotive is one of 50 examples based at Toton but dedicated to Yorkshire traffic at the time of writing. *John S. Whiteley*
Pentax SP1000 85mm Takumar Kodachrome 64 1/250 f6.3

Left: Eighty-five out of the total fleet of Class 56 locomotives were constructed at Doncaster Works, with production lasting from 1977 to 1982. One of the final Doncaster batch, No 56096, is pictured in the confines of the Works on 2 August 1981, shortly before receiving its top coat of paint and being released to traffic. *Bob Osborne*
Canon AE1 50mm Canon Kodachrome 64 1/250 f5.6-8

Above: In late 1988 there were nine scheduled MGR services a day over the East Coast main line north of York, bringing Durham coal to CEGB power stations in the Aire Valley. In practice, however, train frequency varies considerably from week to week, in line with CEGB requirements. A train of northbound return empties is illustrated at Beningbrough, just outside York, on a wintry 28 November 1985, with traction provided by Class 56 No 56128. *David Stacey Pentax K1000 50mm Pentax Kodachrome 64 1/250 f5.6*

Left: Two-tone liveried No 56013 approaches the site of Rogerstone station, on the Western Valleys line near Newport, with an evening MGR service from Oakdale on 14 June 1988. On the left can be seen part of the disused Rogerstone power station.
Michael Mensing
Bronica S2A   75mm Nikkor
Agfachrome 100RS   1/800 f4.5

EDINBURGH
200 MILES

Above: Still in original unadorned blue livery, No 56079 heads south on the up fast line between Shipton and York with a MGR coal working on 31 May 1985. The coal is destined for the Aire Valley, but the locomotive will be detached after arrival in York staging sidings and return north on the next train of empties. In the distance is a further consignment of power station coal, also hauled by a Class 56 locomotive. *J. S. Mattison*
Canon AE1 100mm Kodachrome 64 1/250 f4.5

Left: A comparison of livery styles at Black Carr, on the East Coast main line south of Doncaster. 'Large logo'-liveried No 56125 stands at the head of a southbound loaded MGR working, whilst 'large logo' Railfreight grey-liveried No 56017 passes by on the main line. The photograph is dated 17 September 1985.
Gavin Morrison
Pentax SV 50mm
Kodachrome 25 1/250 f3.5

Above: The infrequent 09.23 SO Bat & Ball (Sevenoaks)-Mountsorrel empty stone train is pictured approaching Clapham Junction on 7 February 1987, hauled by Class 56 No 56076. This machine was one of Gateshead's original Class 56 fleet and was named *Blyth Power* in 1981, but the name was transferred to sister locomotive No 56134 when No 56076 moved south to Toton in September 1986. *Chris Wilson*
Nikon FE 135mm Nikkor Kodachrome 64
1/250 f5.6

Below: Railfreight-liveried locomotive No 56051 draws its train forward through the discharge pit at Thorney Mill (West Drayton) on 19 February 1987. The bogie hopper wagons and terminal facilities at Thorney Mill were intended originally for traffic from Bardon Hill (Leicestershire), but a second flow of stone from the Mendips was quickly established, and the train pictured here was scheduled to proceed empty from Frome after discharge. Thorney Mill is the present limit of working on the former Staines West branch from West Drayton. *Paul Shannon*
Olympus OM1 50mm Zuiko Kodachrome 64
1/250 f5.6

Left: No 56031 *Merehead* heads west near Fairwood Junction, Westbury, with a rake of empty ARC tipplers for Whatley on 28 August 1987. The name *Merehead* was applied in late 1983, at a time when Class 56s held a virtual monopoly on stone trains from both Merehead and Whatley. Who would have thought then that half their duties would soon be appropriated by privately-owned machines from the USA?
John Hillmer
Bronica ETRS 75mm Zenzanon
Fujichrome 100 1/500 f8

Right: With over a decade of service behind it, BR's first 'second generation' diesel freight locomotive, No 56001, powers the 07.20 Whatley-Wolverton ARC stone train along the Oxford-Bletchley line near Bicester on 6 August 1988. This was the first Class 56 to receive Railfreight Construction sub-Sector markings.
John Chalcraft
Olympus OM2 50mm Zuiko
Fujichrome RD100 1/500 f5.6

Above: At Westbury depot on 31 August 1987, Nos 56043 (left) and 56049 (right) share siding accommodation with Class 47 locomotive No 47121. No 56049 had just been embellished with its red bodyside band, bringing further livery variation to an already multifarious fleet! *Geoff Cann Pentax 6×7 Ektachrome 100 1/125 F11*

Right: Just ex-works, No 56062 stands outside Doncaster TMD on 1 April 1986, alongside Class 08 shunter No 08734. No 56062 achievéd fame of a somewhat ignominious nature in July 1988 when it left the rails at Copyhold Junction whilst working the Whatley-Ardingly stone train and ended up at the foot of an embankment. *Gavin Morrison Pentax SV 50mm Kodachrome 25 1/250 f4*

Right: One of Bath Road's small fleet of Class 56s, No 56039, approaches Bedlam Tunnel (at the start of the Whatley branch) on 29 July 1986, heading a smart rake of Procor bogie tipplers for reloading at the ARC quarry. Maintenance responsibility for this and other Mendip stone locomotives was transferred from Bath Road to Cardiff Canton in October 1987, in line with BR's policy of concentrating traction spares and expertise at fewer separate locations.
Michael Mensing
Bronica S2A   75mm Nikkor
Agfa 100RS   1/500 f5.6

Above: Prior to the arrival of Foster Yeoman's four Class 59 locomotives in early 1986, the company's heaviest train, an overnight working from Merehead to Purfleet, was regularly hauled by two Class 56 locomotives. With matching 'large logo' livery, Nos 56049 and 56036 make an impressive sight as they cross Hungerford Common with the return empties from Purfleet on 24 April 1985.

Hugh Dady
Nikkormat FT2 85mm Nikkor Kodachrome 64
1/500 f4

Above: The only Class 56 operation on the 'Coastway' line is the daily stone train from Whatley to Ardingly, together with return empties. Over the years this train has accrued an unfortunate reputation for mishaps of one kind or another, culminating in the spectacular derailment of No 56062 in July 1988. All was well on 11 June 1987, however, when No 56034 was photographed cross-ing Wallington viaduct, near Fareham, with the 09.45 empties from Ardingly. *D. J. Kemp Nikon FE 50mm Nikkor Kodachrome 64 1/250 f5.6*

Below: No 56071 heads the 12.25 Freightliner service from Birmingham Lawley Street to Southampton Maritime Container Terminal over the freight-only line between Aston and Stechford on 22 February 1986. This is a Saturdays-only working which still runs at the time of writing, albeit no longer with Class 56 haulage. *Paul Shannon Olympus OM1 100mm Zuiko Kodachrome 64 1/250 f5.6*

Below: One working which sometimes brought a Class 56 to the Manchester-Sheffield line in 1987 was the containerised petfood train from Melton Mowbray to Ardwick. No 56045 was in charge on 23 April of that year and is pictured taking the Guide Bridge line at Romiley. At that time the train was identified by the reporting number 6Z41, the letter 'Z' denoting a special service, since it had not yet been incorporated into BR's regular freight schedule. *John Hillmer*
Bronica ETRS 75mm Zenzanon Fujichrome 100 1/250 f8

Right: No 56129 climbs the bank from Shotton towards Hawarden on 5 July 1984, heading the 4S49 steel coil empties from Dee Marsh to Mossend. This train was diverted to run via Hawarden and Wrexham (reverse) after closure of the Dee Marsh-Mickle Trafford line on 14 May of the same year. Buoyant traffic levels led to the reopening of the Mickle Trafford line from 1 September 1986, however, and since that date the Scottish coil trains have no longer needed to run via Wrexham.
David Rapson
Canon AE1 135mm Canon Kodachrome 64 1/250 f5.6-8

Above: No 56103 climbs through the Pennines between Saddleworth and Diggle on a beautifully crisp 24 January 1987, heading the 10.18 Runcorn (Folly Lane)-Haverton Hill chemicals train. This is one of a handful of trans-Pennine freight services which continued to run via Diggle after most services were diverted via Hebden Bridge in summer 1985. *John S. Whiteley*

Pentax SP1000 85mm Takumar Fujichrome 50 1/250 f3.5-4

Below: A regular Class 56 duty for several years was the thrice-weekly cement train from Penyffordd to Birmingham (Curzon Street). On 27 March 1986, freshly repainted No 56041 enters Wellington station on the down through line with 6J65, the 12.45 return empties from Curzon Street. Some of the tanks had just been collected from the Castle Cement siding at Oakengates, where 6J65 is scheduled to make a call. *Mick Hemming Pentax ME Super 135mm Takumar Ilfochrome 100 1/500 f5.6*

Right: 'Large logo'-liveried Class 56 No 56102 passes Buxworth on 22 March 1983 with a trainload of Midlands coal for export through Garston Docks. In 1988 these trains no longer ran through the Hope Valley but were routed via Derby, Stoke and the West Coast main line; and the HBA hopper wagons illustrated here have now been displaced by the HAA type used for MGR working.
Rodney Lissenden
Pentax 6×7 105mm Takumar
Fujichrome 100 1/500 f4.5

Above: The 14.23 empty tank train from Leeds to Stanlow (code 7M35) passes Smithy Bridge on 18 September 1986, headed by Class 56 No 56069. This locomotive has since been repainted in Railfreight Coal sub-Sector livery and allotted to the Yorkshire Coal pool, whilst the Stanlow oil trains are now generally in the hands of Class 47 traction. *Paul Shannon*
Olympus OM1 100mm Zuiko Kodachrome 64
1/250 f4-5.6

Above: Dwarfed by the imposing mechanical signalbox at Wrawby Junction, just west of Barnetby, No 56025 heads towards Immingham with a rake of empty 100-tonne oil tanks on 12 March 1987. *John S. Whiteley*
Pentax SP1000 55mm Takumar Fujichrome 50 1/500 f4

Right: The newly applied red bodyside stripe stands out prominently on Class 56 No 56049 as it passes Pangbourne with the 16.10 Theale-Llandarcy empty tank train on 19 August 1987. No 56049 has been based at Cardiff Canton since 1983, and at the time of writing is allocated to the Western Region aggregates pool. *David Moulden*

Nikkormat FT2 50mm Nikkor Kodachrome 25 1/500 f3

Far left: Between 1979 and 1988, pairs of Class 56 locomotives were rostered for the Port Talbot-Llanwern iron ore trains. These were once BR's heaviest freight trains, each with a payload of 2,316 tonnes and consisting of 30 PTA tippler wagons. On 15 June 1983, Nos 56036 and 56041 prepare to depart from BSC Llanwern with an afternoon train of empties. No 56036 became BR's pioneer 'large logo'-liveried locomotive upon receiving a repaint at Stratford in summer 1978; it retained this livery until spring 1988. *David Moulden*
Nikkormat FT2   135mm Nikkor
Kodachrome 25   1/500 f3

Left: No 56036 is pictured again after its latest repaint in Railfreight Petroleum livery, this time double-heading a train of Llanwern-Port Talbot empties together with sister locomotive No 56032. The location is the south portal of Hillfield Tunnel, west of Newport, and the date is 14 June 1988. *Michael Mensing*
Bronica S2A   75mm Nikkor
Agfa 100RS   1/1000 f4.5

Below: After the cessation of steel making at Shotton in 1980, the remaining stockpiled iron ore was taken to Llanwern in a daily trainload of PTA tippler wagons. Class 56 locomotives Nos 56046 and 56033 are pictured at the start of their long journey south on 17 September 1980, running as 6X51 10.10 Shotwick Sidings-Llanwern. The 'X' headcode was used between Shotton and Wrexham because these trains were heavier than normally would be permitted over Hawarden Bridge and were classed as an exceptional load. To the right of the picture lies the former Stewarts & Lloyds plant, the site of which is now occupied by Deeside Titanium.
David Rapson
Praktica L 50mm Agfa CT18 1/250 f5.6-8

Above: Class 56-hauled Speedlink workings are an increasingly rare sight on BR, now that sectorisation is being fully implemented with the consequent allocation of most '56s' to specific coal and aggregates flows. In 1986, however, the daily Bescot-Oxford Speedlink was rostered for Class 56 haulage, and No 56066 is seen nearing its destination with this service on 18 June of that year.

Chris Wilkinson
Nikon F3   85mm Nikkor   Kodachrome 25
1/500 f2.8

Above: Class 56 motive power is provided for the daily Cawoods containerised coal train from Lynemouth to Ellesmere Port, in contrast to the Class 37s which work the company's other services from South Wales. 'Large-logo'-liveried locomotive No 56107 is about to depart from Lynemouth with the 6Z59 'special' to Ellesmere Port on 16 July 1987. Traction for these trains is provided from the same pool that covers local workings in the North East. *Michael Rhodes*
Canon AE1 50mm Canon Kodachrome 64
1/250 f4-5.6

Right: A serene setting for a heavy freight locomotive: Class 56 No 56103 crosses the Chester-field Canal, just east of Worksop, between MGR duties on 2 April 1986. *Les Nixon*
Pentax 6×7 105mm Takumar Ektachrome 100
1/500 f4.5

Left: On 20 August 1983 a DAA railtour from London produced three Class 56s for haulage, Nos 56036, 56045 and 56052. Here the railtour is just about to depart from the picturesque location of Tondu in the care of No 56045, a locomotive then more usually employed on Port Talbot-Llanwern iron ore trains or other Western Region freight services.
John Chalcraft
Mamiya 645   210mm Sekor
Agfa R100S   1/250 f8

Right: Presenting a smart appearance in BR's earlier Railfreight grey livery, Class 56 No 56079 heads south past Ferryhill with a departmental test train on 16 July 1986. This location has since been transformed by overhead electrification masts and wires.
Paul Shannon
Olympus OM1   100mm Zuiko
Kodachrome 64
1/250 f5.6

Above: An impromptu exhibition of BR traction was mounted at London Paddington on Sunday 29 June 1986, to accompany a locally arranged book fair. One of the locomotives displayed was Class 56 No 56037 *Richard Trevithick*, photographed here together with newly refurbished Class 37/5 No 37510, Class 50 No 50023 and green Class 47/4 No 47500 *Great Western*. *Hugh Dady*
Nikkormat FT2 85mm Nikkor Kodachrome 64
1/4 f5.6

Above: No 56112 undergoes a service at Gateshead depot on the evening of 3 November 1987. This was shortly after Gateshead's allocation of '56s' had been officially transferred to Toton, as a prelude to the rundown and eventual closure of the north eastern depot. *Barry Nicolle*
Olympus OM1   50mm Zuiko   Fujichrome 100
20sec f11

Above: Class 56 No 56015 heads south near Colton, between York and Leeds, with an unscheduled Freightliner working on 30 January 1987. This locomotive later became one of the first to receive two-tone grey livery with Coal sub-Sector markings, having also carried the earlier mid-grey Railfreight livery for a time. *David Stacey*
Pentax K1000 100mm Pentax Kodachrome 25
1/250 f3.5

Left: During 1987 the Saturdays-only Freightliner working from Birmingham Lawley Street to Southampton was regularly hauled by a Class 58 locomotive for most of its journey. No 58001 was in charge on 28 March of that year and is pictured approaching Pang-bourne, between Didcot and Reading. In 1988 all Southampton-bound Freightliners are rostered for Class 47 haulage.
Barry Plues
Pentax SP1000 55mm
Kodachrome 64
1/500 f2.8

Left: Railtourers savour the fumes from Class 56 No 56044 as it pulls away from a signal check at Dr Day's Junction, Bristol, hauling the Birmingham-bound 'Paxman Collier' on 12 August 1984. *Ian Gould*
Pentax 6×7 105mm Takumar
Agfachrome R100S 1/250 f5.6

Above: A rare combination of Class 58 No 58002 and Class 86/2 No 86220 *Goliath* has just arrived at Nuneaton on 23 April 1984 with the 07.30 Manchester Piccadilly-London Euston express. This was an Easter Monday, when certain West Coast main line services were being diverted via Birmingham and Nuneaton due to the remodelling of Rugby station. The Class 58 in this instance returned light to Saltley depot after arrival at Nuneaton. *Paul Biggs*
Olympus OM10 80-210mm Tamron zoom
Agfachrome 200 1/250 f8

Below: Fly ash trains run from Ratcliffe and West Burton power stations to disposal points at Fletton (Peterborough) and Little Barford (near St Neots). Class 58 No 58010 approaches Barrow-on-Soar with 6M46, the 15.35 Fletton-Ratcliffe empties on 24 April 1985. The CSA wagons used on these trains are similar in design to the now withdrawn CPV Presflo cement wagons, but have a longer wheelbase and superstructure. *Bob Osborne Canon AE-1 100mm Canon Kodachrome 64 1/500 f4*

Above: It is not unusual for CEGB coal traffic to keep flowing at weekends and on bank holidays when demand for electricity production or fuel restocking is high. Here Class 58 No 58035 passes the GWR signalbox to the north of Banbury station with 7V49, the 08.44 Baddesley-Didcot MGR working, on Bank Holiday Monday 29 August 1988. *Paul Shannon*
Olympus OM1 50mm Zuiko Kodachrome 64 1/500 f4-5.6

Left: Class 58 No 58034 crosses the River Avon at Leek Wootton, between Leamington Spa and Coventry, with a Didcot-Three Spires Junction empty MGR service on 5 May 1987. This locomotive was named *Bassetlaw* at Worksop in December 1985. *Colin Underhill*
Mamiya 645 Fujichrome 100 1/1000 f2.8

Above: In 1984 a daytime Speedlink service operated from Toton to Ashburys and back, often bringing Class 58 haulage to the Manchester area. On 18 September of that year, No 58006 was in charge, and is pictured passing Fairfield with the southbound working, 7M60 12.46 Ashburys-Toton. Since that date both Ashburys and Toton have ceased to function as main Speedlink yards, with most of their work transferred to Warrington and Derby St Marys respectively. *Kim Fullbrook*
Canon AE-1 35-70mm Canon zoom
Kodachrome 64 1/250 f5.6

49

Left: No 58043 approaches Worksop with an afternoon eastbound MGR working on 16 September 1986. *Andrew Fell*
Pentax Spotmatic
50mm Takumar
Kodachrome 25 1/500 f2.8

Right: Just leaving Ratcliffe power station on 3 August 1987 is Class 58 No 58010 with 6E54, the 11.57 fly ash train to Fletton. *Andrew Fell*
Mamiya 645J 80mm Sekor C
Ektachrome 64
1/250 f5.6

Above: Barrow Hill interior: Class 58 Nos 58034 *Bassetlaw*, 58039 *Rugeley Power Station* and 58006 stand around the turntable at this former steam shed on 27 September 1987. *Alistair Jolly Nikon FM2 90mm Tamron Kodachrome 64 1/15 f5.6*

Above: Barrow Hill exterior: Nos 58049 *Littleton Colliery*, 58043 and 58037 await their next turn of duty in the depot yard on 2 August 1987.

Stewart Jolly
*Pentax MX 50mm Pentax Kodachrome 64
1/250 f5.6-8*

Right: No 58018 heads north past Toton yard with a rake of empty BDA bogie bolster wagons on 24 April 1985. This was shortly after the end of the long miners' strike, when coal traffic was still at a low ebb, and Toton '56s' and '58s' were being used on a wide variety of miscellaneous freight duties. *Geoff Cann*
Pentax MX 135mm Pentax
Kodachrome 64 1/250 f5.6

Above: Washwood Heath sidings are used as a staging point for MGR trains between the Midlands coalfield and Didcot power station. On 3 July 1987 Class 58 No 58040 *Cottam Power Station* pulls away from the yard with empties for Daw Mill Colliery, which will later form a 'special' 7Z60 13.00 Daw Mill-Didcot service. *Paul Shannon Olympus OM1 50mm Zuiko Kodachrome 64 1/250 f5.6-8*

Left: Ex-works Class 58 No 58041 *Ratcliffe Power Station* glides past the massive opencast coal loading point at Bennerley, on the Erewash Valley line, with an MGR rake of standard HAA wagons on 30 January 1987. The vantage point for this photograph is the viaduct of former Great Northern and Midland Railway route to Derby.
David Moulden
Nikkormat FT2 50mm Nikkor
Kodachrome 25
1/500 f2.4

Right: Coal trains from Bolsover, Markham and Oxcroft Collieries are normally routed via Seymour Junction and Barrow Hill, at which point longer-distance trains (eg to Didcot) may be held over. The alternative route from Seymour across to Elmton and Creswell now sees little use except for light locomotive movements. On 16 September 1986, No 58027 takes the curve to Barrow Hill at Hall Lane Junction with loaded HAAs from Markham Colliery.
Alistair Jolly
Fujica STX1 50mm Fujinon
Kodachrome 64
1/250 f5.6-8

Left: At busy periods, incoming trains at Didcot power station may have to wait in the arrival sidings for previous services to complete their discharge. Such an occasion is depicted here on 6 November 1986, as Nos 58017 and 58012 stand side by side in the sidings parallel to the main line. Some 14 trainloads of coal are scheduled to arrive at Didcot on a typical working day, mostly from the Midlands and South Yorkshire. *Barry Nicolle Olympus OM1 50mm Zuiko Fujichrome 100 1/250 f8*

Above: No 58020 *Doncaster Works — BRE* eases across Shireoaks East Junction into Worksop Up Yard on 21 October 1987 whilst working 7F53, the 10.00 Ollerton Colliery-Cottam MGR service. This locomotive was the first of its class to be named, and received the honour at Doncaster Works itself on 7 November 1984. *Barry Nicolle Olympus OM1 135mm Zuiko Fujichrome 100 1/500 f5.6*

59

Left: On 20 September 1986 Hertfordshire Rail-tours ran an enthusiasts' special from London King's Cross to the Lincolnshire coast, hauled throughout by heavy freight machine No 58039 *Rugeley Power Station*. This locomotive had, along with Nos 58040-2, received its name earlier in the same month. The tour itinerary included visits to both Skegness and Cleethorpes, the first time that a Class 58 had reached either of these locations. The combination of a circuitous route and a bright sunny day provided the railway photographer with some

excellent opportunities to record the event, and in this view No 58039 is seen ambling along the Skegness branch near Little Steeping, en route for Cleethorpes. *Douglas Johnson*
Mamiya 645 1000S 80mm Mamiya
Agfachrome 100RS (rated at 100 ASA)
1/500 f6.3

Above: In connection with the proposed 'super pit' at Hawkhurst Moor, near Kenilworth, a pro-motional exercise was mounted by Railfreight Coal

during July 1988, in which local dignitaries were conveyed by VIP saloon around the district. The 'tour' is seen here on 16 July behind newly reliveried Class 58 No 58002 *Daw Mill Colliery*. It is passing the site of Kenilworth Junction, which is the likely starting point of a BR branch to the proposed pit. *Colin Underhill*
Mamiya 645 1000S 80mm Mamiya
Fujichrome 100 1/500 f5.6

Right: No 58025 is pictured under construction in Doncaster No 2 Bay on 20 November 1984. This was the 2,517th locomotive to be constructed at the Works, with just a further 25 remaining to be built. It was outshopped in January 1985 but not released to revenue-earning traffic until two months later. *Colin Marsden*
Nikon FM2 50mm Nikkor Kodachrome 64 1/4 f8

Left: The launch of Railfreight's new identity on 15 October 1987 was marked by a display of locomotives in the new colour schemes at Ripple Lane depot. Both Classes 56 and 58 were represented, and this view shows a resplendent No 58050 proclaiming its allegiances by means of the Coal sub-Sector logo, the Toton depot badge (cooling towers) and even the name *Toton Traction Depot.* Unfortunately No 58050 disgraced itself during the display by refusing to emerge from Ripple Lane shed under its own power, and had to be pushed out by an adjacent Class 37. *Hugh Ballantyne*
Leica M4-2 50mm Summicron Kodachrome 25 1/60 f2.8-4

Below: Another immaculate Class 58, No 58002, poses outside Doncaster Major Depot on 11 February 1988, having just received its first classified overhaul and a repaint in the new Railfreight Coal colours. *Barry Nicolle*
Olympus OM1   55mm   Fujichrome 100   1/125 f11

Overleaf: Hawthorn blossom enhances the setting for Class 58 No 58018 as it rolls down Hatton bank with an up Didcot MGR on 4 June 1986.
Peter Tandy
Olympus OM1   100mm Zuiko   Ektachrome 100   1/500 f4